Southern California

out & about

All photos by John Eng unless otherwise noted
Book designed by John Eng
Type set in Myriad Pro

ISBN: 978-0-7643-4071-0
Printed in China

On the Cover: Mount Whitney, at 14,495 feet above sea level, is the highest mountain in the lower 48. The surreal landscape of Alabama Hills in the foreground can be seen in countless movies, from *Gunga Din* (1939) to *Gladiator* (2000) to more recently, *Transformers: Revenge of the Fallen* (2009) and *Terminator Salvation* (2009).

Southern California

out & about

John Eng & Adriene Biondo

Mono

Fresno

Inyo

Tulare

Kings

3

4

San Luis
Obispo

2

Kern

Santa
Barbara

San Bernardino

Ventura

Los
Angeles

1

Orange

Riverside

5

San Diego

Imperial

N Southern California Counties

S I E R R A   N E V A D A

CONTENTS

Film students at Griffith Park recreating a scene from Ed Wood's infamous low-budget, sci-fi film *Plan 9 from Outer Space*. Mixing old technology with new, they're shooting a paper plate flying saucer hung on a stick via fishing line with a modern hi-def digital camera.

FOREWORD

They are tiny specs of light, prismatically dancing with molecules of water, yet rainbows suggest something enormous: imagination.

For those millions of people who have lived, visited, or even had daydreams of Southern California, they have pursued and even found their rainbows.

We are playfully reviled as the "land of fruits and nuts," but it's really the land of no excuses. If it's not here, it's not anywhere. If such a place exists to find oneself, this is it.

The Prometheus of local broadcasting, silver-haired Jerry Dunphy, opened the "Big News," with "From the desert to the sea, to all of Southern California." These are the parameters of our "Superstate" of which the ancient Athenians and Romans could only have dreamed. We have it all. More importantly, where it counts, we have it less. It's obvious we canoe Lake Arrowhead at dawn and surf Malibu at noon. Less obvious, but more essential to our character than our diverse geography, are the psychological encumbrances from which we are free. Unlike Europe and most of America, we are not slavishly reverent to tradition.

Even the most emblematic symbols of Southern California, the automobile and cinema, are not indigenous. Like most everything else, they too are European immigrants who floated across the cold Atlantic and the Great Plains to bask in the mist of our rainbow. We are amused and even infatuated by these welcomed visitors, but not paralyzed from independent thought by the dreary idolatry attached to native birth. Although our heritage reaches past the greedy nuggets of the Gold Rush, past the pious adobe Missions of Father Serra, much of its character was abruptly redefined in the smoldering post-WWI era.

The Los Angeles City Hall, springing from the "Roaring 20s," is the titular capitol building of this "Superstate." Its triangular crown pierces the rainbow with a portrait so distinctive that it is recognizable to citizens from anywhere in the galaxy. Its charisma is enriched with starring roles in reruns of *Perry Mason*, *Dragnet*, and *Mission Impossible*. Officially, "Superstate" status was conferred one day in the 1950s. The producers of George Reeves' *Superman* television show, in the second season, chose our city hall as the headquarters of the *Daily Planet*. Suddenly we became the epicenter of not only imagination but of "Truth, Justice and the American Way."

City Hall is not our only architectural tent pole, which slices through the neoclassical and Gothic malaise of public structures.

Our center of gravity preens on top of a magnificent urban wilderness.

The three, copper-skinned domes of the Griffith Observatory, like a laboratory out of a Jules Verne novel, benignly glow over the city like a benevolent Art Deco monarch.

Of the world's spectacular perches, none is more romantic than this hillside sanctuary. To the South, L.A.'s ziggurated skyline twinkles intoxicating visual melodies; to the west, the rambling Route 66 plays its finale at the Pacific Ocean.

To the northwest, blazing a message like a frozen comet, the most august of all landmarks, the precise location of the end of the rainbow. Contrary to the myth, there is something here more valuable than a pot of gold.

While the Eiffel Tower and the Golden Gate Bridge showcase monumental engineering and artistic achievements, the grandeur of this relatively humble billboard is not derived from its physical attributes. At only 45 feet tall, its size is modest. Its craftsmanship, at best, is adequate. Its electrifying strength surges from the colossal idea it represents. Emblazoned with the letters H-O-L-L-Y-W-O-O-D, this sign symbolizes the awesome power of the collective imaginations of all past, present, and future civilizations.

Found in this photographic essay is an ambitious selection of majestic and quirky photos, detailing off-the-beaten path, and roadside findings. The descriptions are scholarly and sometimes verging on poetic. Southern California's imaginative spirit is also captured in the presentation of the material. While the safer approach is simply to plop images and text into a template, they have chosen a bolder path of extracting the flavor the content and sprayed its essence on the page with counterpointing and complementary textures, giving each layout a unique character.

Frank!
Publisher of *Collector Magazine* for 30 Years

Photo by Frank.

INTRODUCTION

While driving into a thunderstorm up San Jacinto Mountain, this photo was taken looking back in the direction we were coming from, towards L.A. A few minutes later, rain began to pour buckets as the rain cloud engulfed us, visibility so shallow that we could barely see the front of our car.

A THIN SLICE OF CALIFORNIA HISTORY

California existed as the Land of Dreams even before it was an actual place. Shortly after Columbus "discovered" the New World, around 1510, Spanish writer Garcia Ordonez de Montalvo wrote the popular novel *Las Sergas de Esplandian* in which he describes California as "a mythical island just right of the Indies." For the next one hundred years, the Baja Peninsula became the island known as California.

In 1701, Jesuit Father Kino moved into the Baja Region after establishing missions in what is now known as Arizona and Mexico. His life mission would be denied by Carlos III of Madrid who revoked Father Kino's powers and placed him under arrest. The religious conversion and missionary work would later be completed by Father Junipero Serra, of the Franciscan Order, who established missions within one day's horseback ride apart, all along the California coastline.

Colonization did not begin until 1769, when under Russian competition, Spain established San Diego under Governor Gaspar de Portola.

Just three months before the East Coast colonies claimed independence from King George III on July 4th, 1776, Spain sent Juan Bautista de Anza to colonize San Francisco with nearly 250 men, women, and children, along with mules, horses, and cattle. Now 234 years after the initial discovery, the Spanish were ready to exploit the New World. It appears that Spain started too late because only 46 years remained before Mexico would gain their independence, and 22 years after that, Mexico would become part of the United States of America.

Gold was discovered east of Sacramento in 1848. As the world converged on California there was a sudden population explosion with empty ships littering the San Francisco harbor. In 1849, General Andres Pico surrendered to Lieutenant-Colonel John Charles Fremont and the following year California became a part of the United States. As rich East Coast vacationers became attracted to the climate, beauty, and investment possibilities of the West, the railroad companies of the country expanded their reach and along came the Southern Pacific, the Santa Fe, and the Union Pacific railroads, making access easier. And since the Mediterranean climate of California is ideal for farming, agriculture quickly became a major industry. Oil was discovered in the 1880s, sparking another population boom on top of the previous boom. Culture came with writers like Samuel Clements, Robert Louis Stevenson, and Jack London; while universities, libraries, opera houses, and theaters opened everywhere in the state. Natural and man-made seaports in San Francisco, Los Angeles, San Diego, and other cities made California a natural trading center. Soon manufacturing would become another major industry in the state, including ships, automobiles, and aircraft. And even before World War I, Hollywood was well on its way to becoming the movie capital of the world.

Late afternoon at Sequoia National Park, near Lodgepole.

NATURAL RESOURCES

Natural resources range from minerals such as gold, silver, and copper, to energy-producing resources like oil and natural gas, with lumber, cement, and other building materials.

Temperatures can range from minus 56°F to 134°F, but most of California is mild and pleasant all year around. The state contains deserts, mountains, valleys, canyons, rivers, lakes, and 1,200 miles of coastline along the Pacific Ocean. There is an abundance of every conceivable resource except for one, water. Although much of the state's supply of fresh water comes from the Sierra Nevada mountain range, it has to be transported to the cities and farmlands via aqueducts, canals, tunnels, and pumping stations.

For natural beauty and diversity, California is unmatched. The 400- by roughly 80-mile Sierra Nevada mountain range includes National Parks like Yosemite, Kings Canyon, and Sequoia. Outside of the Sierras, there are Desert Parks such as Death Valley, Joshua Tree, and Anza-Borrego. In total, there are eight National Parks, 18 National Forests, countless Wildernesses, and 278 State Parks and Beaches (or more than 1.5 million acres) in California. Natural fauna includes California grizzly bears, brown bears, black bears, bighorn sheep, tule elk, many different types of trout, a large variety of fish, and the California condor, the largest land bird in North America with a wing span of 10 feet.

INDUSTRIES

The following are just a few of the state's industries: agriculture, mining , logging, shipping, real estate, entertainment, tourism, medical, defense, aviation, science, education, hi-tech, sports, and recreation. In 1993, California surpassed Wisconsin in the production of dairy products and is in fact, now number one in the United States.

During World War II, industries across America were put to work in an all-out effort to win the war. California built ships and aircraft, hiring tens of thousands of workers in round-the-clock shifts. The demand for workers created yet another population explosion and the infrastructure needed for all these workers, such as housing and transportation.

THE AUTOMOBILE

The railroads built in the late 1880s promoted comfortable, convenient, and inexpensive travel within the U.S. Around this time, there was a national movement to "See America First." Then, after World War I, various automobile clubs across the country promoted travel within the U.S. via the automobile. One such group was the National Park to Park Highway Association, which sold the American Public on touring the great National Parks of the U.S. by driving to them. Along with the car, came the "Good Road Movement" of the 1920s, which encouraged and lobbied for the construction of safe roads and highways.

Since it is impossible to include everything in Southern California, we tried to represent something from each region, knowing full well that it is seen through the prism of our eyes. Although Mono County is technically considered a part of Northern California, we decided to make this one exception so that we may share with you some of our most beautiful images of the Sierra Nevada.

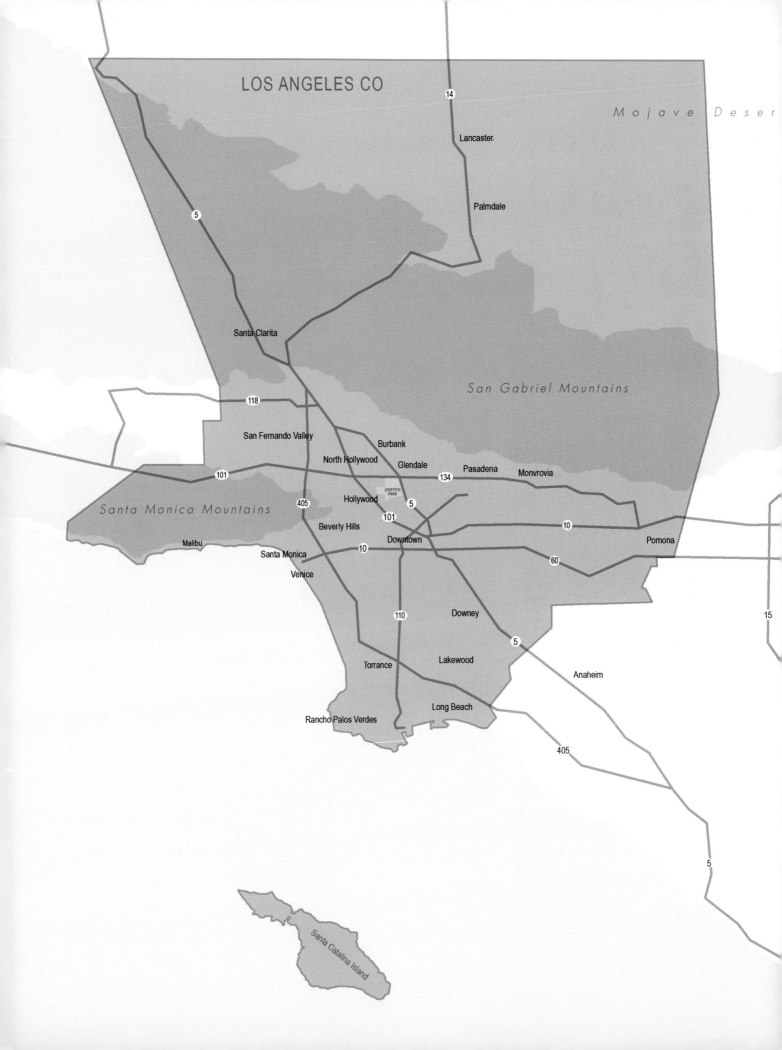

1 Los Angeles

View of Downtown L.A. from the Mulholland Drive overlook, with Hollywood and the Capitol Records building prominent in the foreground. The smog was being pushed out by two days of rain and wind.

1st Street Bridge, Downtown L.A. City Hall is just to the right of the setting sun.

LOS ANGELES

"Set in a region more desert than oasis, it is a man-made gigantic improvisation that grew in spite of its location rather than because of it."

–Annette Welles
The Los Angeles Guide Book, 1972

"Almost anything you can say about Los Angeles is true. It's large; it's a mess; it lives; it's vulgar; it's beautiful. For L.A. represents, more than any other city, the fulfillment of the American Dream...of wealth, speed, freedom, mobility."

–Reyner Banham
Los Angeles, The Architecture of Four Ecologies, 1971

"So Los Angeles is crude, corny, mixed and nondescript, yet a mecca for artistic and highly skilled persons of a hundred kinds, who have freckled its broad and homely face with loveliness and wonder."

–Lee Shippey
The Los Angeles Book, 1950

Los Angeles, with over 80 municipalities, is listed as the eighth largest economy in the world, compared with other countries—not just cities. The list of industries goes on and on: from entertainment (Hollywood) to science (aerospace, JPL, Cal Tech) to shipping (Ports of Long Beach and San Pedro), education (numerous colleges and universities), medicine, tourism, agriculture, etc. Oil is still being pumped 24/7 all over the city, even in residential backyards. It is a thriving, diverse urban center of the world that continues to reinvent itself.

Los Angeles is known as the "Creative Capital of the World." One in every six residents works in a creative industry. Even if the writer, artist, or musician does not settle here permanently, a pilgrimage is usually in order. All types of architecture can be found here, including indigenous styles that are unique to Southern California, like the ultra-modern style called Googie.

Just as in post World War II, Europe became the Old World and New York represented the Modern City. Now, in a post 2000 world, Los Angeles has become the *new* Modern City, on the cutting edge of what is to come. The world now looks to L.A. as a porthole to the future.

Spidey makes an appearance at the Santa Monica Pier.

The Pacific Wheel at the Santa Monica Pier is solar-powered, 130 feet tall, and turns at 2.5 revolutions per minute. You can get a great view of the coastline on a clear day from the top.

1
Venice Beach Freakshow, a permanent crowd
pleaser of the boardwalk.

2
A boardwalk performer at Venice Beach making a
living doing his thing.

3
Mesmerized by the unrelenting beat, beachgoers
cannot resist dancing to the rhythm of the drum
circle at Venice Beach.

4
One of many perks of living in Southern California
is a free beach on a hot summer afternoon, Santa
Monica.

While the security guard was checking the rear of this Wilshire Boulevard business building, a group of skateboarders stormed the front steps and had their way.

One of the sleek, mid-century modern skyscrapers in Century City. At one time, this area was all part of 20th Century Fox Studios. When Elizabeth Taylor and Richard Burton's *Cleopatra* flopped big time at the box office in 1963, Fox narrowly avoided bankruptcy by selling off acres of their lot. The result is Century City.

Visitors to the Hollywood Bowl are greeted by the enchanting *Muse of Music, Dance, and Drama*
sculpture by George Stanley. This massive piece of granite stands 22 feet tall and 200 feet wide and
doubles as the amphitheater's retaining wall. Stanley also designed the Oscar statue, based on a sketch
done by MGM Art Director Cedric Gibbons.

Griffith Park Observatory and Planetarium, built in 1935 under the Works Progress Administration (WPA), is a Moderne masterpiece, forever immortalized in the 1955 film *Rebel Without a Cause* with James Dean and Natalie Wood.

The Hollywood and Highland Center is modeled after the City of Babylon created in D.W. Griffith's 1916 milestone film, *Intolerance*. From this angle, the Hollywood sign is not only visible but framed by the building (just left of center).

Christmas tree dancers at the festive Hollywood Christmas Parade in front of the Cinerama Dome on Sunset Boulevard.

Parade-crashers on the sidelines of the Hollywood Christmas Parade in front of the Pantages Theater on Hollywood Boulevard.

Opening in 1939, Union Station naturally became a transportation hub for a young and growing city. Architects Donald B. Parkinson and John Parkinson, a father and son team, combined Early Spanish architecture with the modernist aesthetics of the Art Deco Moderne style. The Parkinsons also designed Bullocks Wilshire and Saks Fifth Avenue in L.A. Union Station has been featured in many movies including *Blade Runner* (1982) and *Pearl Harbor* (2001).

The place to rendezvous, the information booth at Union Station. *Photo by Adriene Biondo.*

View of Downtown L.A. showing the Los Angeles Times Building, taken from the top of the 28-story City Hall building.

Beautiful Miss L.A. Chinatown 2011 graced the parade with her presence.

A Chinese deity in bright colors parades down Hill Street to the delight of thousands.

Traditionally, Dragon and Tiger dancers were men, but in the 2012 L.A. Chinatown New Year Parade, women are now just as well represented.

The main Dragon swooped east on Hill Street then back west on Broadway causing spectacular excitement among the viewing crowd.

Fighter jet at George Izay Park in the City of Burbank.

Aerial view of Downtown L.A. City Hall is just right of center, at one time the tallest building in Los Angeles. Fondly referred to as The Superman Building, it stood in for the *Daily Planet* newspaper offices in the 1950s *Superman* television series.

Travel Town Train Museum, Griffith Park, a free and underrated
attraction of the L.A. City Department of Parks and Recreation.

A father shares with his son a romanticized but outdated mode of transportation once referred to as The Iron Horse. Although Travel Town Train Museum opened in 1952, the idea began with Charley Atkins, George Hjelte, and William Frederickson, Jr. (all L.A. Parks and Recreation employees) in 1947.

T R A I N

Carnival rides at the Los Angeles County Fair in Pomona. This fair is so big it would take a full week to see everything. Why rush? Take your time and enjoy.

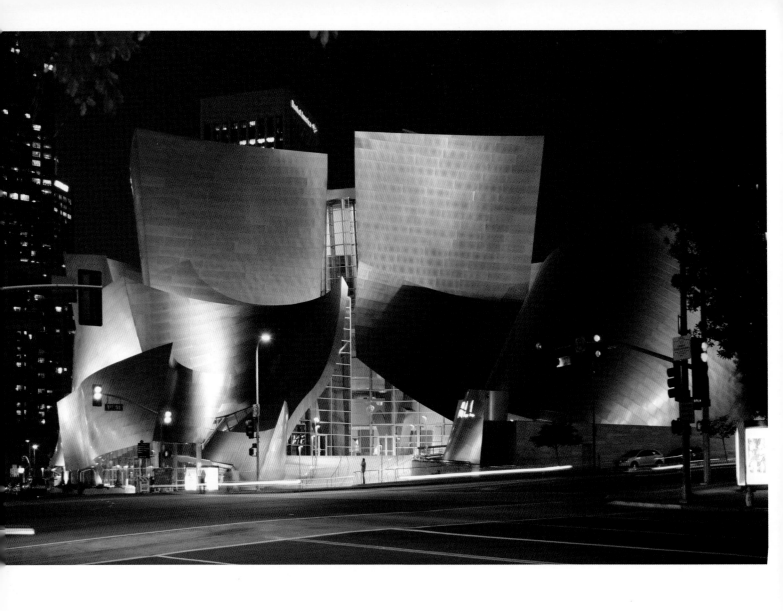

World-renowned, and local, architect Frank O. Gehry's Disney Concert Hall (1988-94) in Downtown L.A. This was actually proposed *before* the Guggenheim in Bilbao, Spain, but was completed after Bilbao, where much of the initial fanfare had already been spent.

Although modest looking, Olvera Street is the oldest street in Los Angeles, and home to the Pico House (1869), oldest house in the city, and Our Lady Queen of the Angels Church (1818).

Here we caught a Mariachi band taking a break between sets.

Post storm sky over Hansen Dam (1940 WPA project), on the border of Pacoima and Lake View Terrace.
Once a thriving summer recreation area in the 1950s and 60s, it was the locals' poor man's Lake Tahoe.

Hawaiian dancers at The Grove, just east of Farmers Market. With a trolley system and Dancing Waters, this new breed of shopping, dining, and entertainment center rivals just about anything in Las Vegas (sans gambling).

OPPOSITE PAGE
Sturtevant Falls in the Angeles National Forest, a popular day hike just north of Arcadia. The falls is on the way to Sturtevant Camp, established in 1897. Along with Harwood Lodge (1930) and numerous other camps and resorts, this region became the center for The Great Hiking Era of the San Gabriel Mountains between 1880-1938.

Leo Carrillo Beach is a part of Malibu's Leo Carrillo State Park, named after the actor, preservationist, and conservationist. This gorgeous park offers 1.5 miles of beach, caves, reefs, and parkland for swimming, diving, surfing, windsurfing, camping, and hiking.

When the water recedes at low tide, sparkling tide pools reveal a variety of sea life, including colorful starfish, mussels, crabs, sea cucumbers, and anemones.

Similar to Point Lobos, Leo Carrillo State Park is a mecca for photographers, campers, surfers, and vacationers. The turbulent relationship between land, wind, and sea is evident everywhere you look. At low tide a surreal terrain reveals sea caves which are just awesome to experience.

An ocean sunset at Naples in Long Beach, aahhh, just another day in paradise.

Previous Pages

1
One of the fantasy cottages in the town of Tujunga, at the base of the San Gabriel Mountains. Indigenous boulder houses can still be found here, built from rocks hand carried from the Big Tujunga Wash.

2
Experimental Airform Bubble House (1946) by architect Wallace Neff, who typically designed homes in the Spanish Medieval and Spanish Colonial Revival styles. Neff's résumé includes the Pickford Estate, homes for Charlie Chaplin and Cary Grant, and other celebrities which can be found along California Street and in East Pasadena.

3
Trianon Apartments (1928), architect Leland A. Bryant, Hollywood. An apartment in the French Chateau style and named after Marie Antoinette's chateau hideaway. The French influence was evoked as returning WWI soldiers brought back stories of the impressive castles and chateaus they had seen in France.

4
Architect John Lautner's Chemosphere House (1960), a symbol of the ultra-sleek modern architecture Los Angeles is now famous for. The Flying Saucer House has appeared in many Hollywood movies such as *Body Double* (1984) and *Charlie's Angels* (2000).

5
1950s apartment living in the City of Downey—home of the Apollo Space Program and the world's oldest operating McDonalds.

6
The Mark Wilshire Tower Apartments (1966), quintessential modern apartment living in what is now Koreatown.

7
In 1978, architect Frank O. Gehry revolutionized architecture with his "deconstructivist" theory when he redesigned his own California bungalow in Santa Monica.

8
This house is an example of the Craftsman style found throughout the city.

9
Castle Green, Pasadena. A unique building, originally the annex to Hotel Green. Architect Frederick L. Roehrig used elements from Moorish, Spanish, Victorian, and other styles to create this Pasadena icon for Col. George G. Green in 1899.

10
The Kahlua, a1960s Polynesian-style apartment building, north of the famous Bahooka restaurant in Rosemead.

11
This fairly recent apartment building near Hollywood and Western, built over the Metro Hollywood line, borrows unapologetically from Mondrian.

12
Platt Office Building (1981). In this architectural mash-up, elements of buildings from Bunker Hill have been reconstituted into a Queen Anne/Victorian-style office building in Winnetka.

13
This stubborn survivor is sandwiched between a stucco box and a commercial brick building near the former site of the Ambassador Hotel.

14
These stilt houses perched off the Hollywood Hills appear to be floating on air. Stepping inside one, you will also *feel* like you're floating on air.

15
A beautiful Pasadena home just off of the Tournament of Roses Parade route near Orange Grove and Colorado Boulevard.

16
1959...the ultimate modern house built in the land of dreams. Case Study House #22 is a seminal steel house designed by modern architect Pierre Koenig for C.H. (Buck) Stahl (*stahl* is German for "steel"). You can get a glimpse in *Marrying Man* (1991) starring Alec Baldwin and Kim Basinger and *Galaxy Quest* (1999) with Tim Allen and Sigourney Weaver.

50

Hills of Simi Valley during the Station Fire. At night the smoke, glow, and flames created a spectacular, though frightening, experience for local residents.

A symbolic reminder of the Station Fire, December 2009. Devastating fires are not uncommon in Southern California, which is often plagued by drought, high temperatures, and strong winds.

Southern California is not only about desert and beaches. Here at Mt. Baldy, during the month of May there was still enough snow left to satisfy local skiers and snowboarders.

Kids dropping off their snowboards. Mt. Baldy Recreation Area, a part of the Angeles National Forest.

Thunder Mountain at 8,587 feet, taken from Mt. Baldy Notch.

Celebrating Halloween at Heritage Square, a petting zoo of rescued Victorian homes and buildings at the end of Homer Street, south of Avenue 43. Were it not for the efforts of preservationists, these one-of-a-kind treasures would have been lost forever.

Families trick-or-treating on Halloween, the biggest holiday in L.A. Entire neighborhoods, like this one in Cypress Park, are set up with animated and live characters, fog machines, spooky music, candy, and lots of fun.

Trick-or-treaters at Heritage Square.

Chinese Garden on the lush grounds of the Huntington Library and Gardens in San Marino, founded in 1919 by wealthy railroad man Henry E. Huntington, who developed the Pacific Electric Red Cars, one of the most successful modes of transportation Los Angeles has ever known. The Huntington Library is one of the finest research libraries in the world.

Even a muffler shop can become famous in L.A. Whittier Boulevard, in industrial East Los Angeles.

Academy Theater (1939) by architect S. Charles Lee. Manchester Boulevard, in Inglewood.
Directly under the flight path of LAX, this Moderne theatre was once a glorious movie
palace that is now operating as a church.

Histo-tainer (historian and entertainer) Charles Phoenix presenting his special 3-D
God Bless Americana slide show at the Downtown Independent Theater.

Animal Cracker Conspiracy delighting children with their "tall tactics" at the Puppetry Festival at the McGroarty Park Recreation Center in Tujunga. *Photo by Adriene Biondo.*

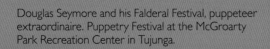

Douglas Seymore and his Falderal Festival, puppeteer extraordinaire. Puppetry Festival at the McGroarty Park Recreation Center in Tujunga.

1

An attendee of the 2010 "Mojave Mile"——here the goal was to have a full mile of vintage cars and hot rods head over to customizing king Gene Winfield's shop in the Mojave Desert, north of Rosamond.

2

Herb Jeffries, the first African-American singing cowboy movie star, here singing at the L.A. Jazz Festival.

3

A beauty contestant at the 2011 Grand National Roadster Show, L.A. County Fairgrounds.

4

Julius Shulman, the Dean of Architectural Photography in L.A. Shulman recorded Los Angeles during a career that spanned nearly a century and became a larger-than-life figure known the world over.

5

Josh Agle, aka *Shag*, a contemporary artist working and living the mid-century modern Tiki lifestyle in L.A.

6

Our waitress at Goody's Coffee Shop, just before they were forced to move out of their original 1950s San Gabriel location.

7

Modern architect Ray Kappe in his home studio. Presently still working, his career started in the early 1950s working for Anshen + Allen in the Bay Area. In 1972 he co-founded SCI-Arc, a leading school of architecture that began in Santa Monica.

8

Ed Lum, a well-known graphic designer who maintains his home and studio in the very first trailer park in L.A. to become a historic landmark.

9

Mason (left) and Charlee Peterson (right) of Long Beach.

10

Our docent, James, made our visit to the Watts Towers truly enjoyable. The Watts Towers are one of the most beloved examples of folk art in L.A., designed and built by Italian immigrant Simon Rodia.

11

Photographer Leland Lee, one time assistant to Julius Shulman. At 92, Leland's still working and going strong! Look him up if you need an architectural photographer.

12

Dutch, aka Steven Vreeken, a regular at Bob's Broiler in Downey, and one of the original cruisers back when it operated as Johnie's Broiler in the 1960s.

As the old song goes, "26 miles across the sea, Santa Catalina is waiting for me...romance, romance..." The island of Catalina is famous for its glass bottom boat rides where searchlight boats go out at night in search of the Amazing Flying Fish! Easier to spot are the bright orange Garibaldi, California's official marine state fish. In the background you can see the gorgeous Catalina Casino/Ballroom (1928) where big bands still play and the Art Deco Society holds its annual soiree. *Photo by Adriene Biondo.*

Dodger Stadium (1962), ultra-cool, mid-century modern home of the
Los Angeles Dodgers and one of the great ballparks in the U.S.

Civil War Reenactment, El Dorado Park, Long Beach. Why do the Confederates always win in these reenactments?

Officers enjoying a relaxing moment with a stogie, off the battlefield.

Although scripted, in the heat of battle, one can easily get lost in the reality of the moment.

The seriousness in each reenactor can easily be read on their faces.

The Christmas window display at Trashy Lingerie, a hip L.A. apparel store located at La Cienega and Waring Ave.

L.A.'s industrial areas are sought-after sites for filming. Here model Brittany Dailey poses for photographer Estevan Oriol and *FreeStyle Rides* magazine in Downtown L.A. Special thanks to Brian Boley for letting us come along while his hot rod was being photographed on this shoot.

2 Central Coast

134
210
10
5
LOS
ANGELES
15
405

5

A Can-Can dancer at
the French Festival in
Santa Barbara.

CENTRAL COAST

"Santa Barbara is a paradise; Disneyland is a paradise; the U.S. is a paradise. Paradise is just paradise. Mournful, monotonous, and superficial though it may be, it is paradise. There is no other."

–Jean Baudrillard

"Halfway between Los Angeles and San Francisco you'll find San Luis Obispo, America's Happiest Town, population 45,000."

–Jenny McCarthy, correspondent for the *Oprah Winfrey Show*, 2010

California's Central Coast is a magnificent natural wilderness that starts north of Ventura reaching up to Southern Monterey Bay and Point Conception. For the purposes of this book, we will be covering Ventura County, Santa Barbara County, and San Luis Obispo County. Vacationers can travel by car, or relax and go by train via Amtrak's Coast Starlight and Pacific Surfliner routes, which serve much of this region.

San Luis Obispo County is the heart of the Central Coast and halfway point between Los Angeles and San Francisco. Nestled in this area of rugged coastlines and spectacular scenery, you will find quaint towns like Cambria, Morro Bay, Pismo Beach, and Paso Robles. Visit historic Hearst Castle at San Simeon, and California Mission San Luis Obispo de Tolosa. With miles of beaches, hiking and recreation areas, concerts, fine art galleries, theaters, shops, restaurants and coffee houses, there is something for everyone. Oh, and a visit to SLO wouldn't be complete without stopping at the always-popular Apple Farm Inn and forever-pink Madonna Inn.

It's no secret why so many people make their home in Santa Barbara and Ventura Counties. Carpinteria, Montecito, Santa Barbara, Summerland, and Ventura are easily some of the most beautiful coastal towns in the world. Known as the "American Riviera," Santa Barbara is a world-class resort with a balmy, Mediterranean climate, sandy beaches, and stunning Spanish architecture. Santa Barbara is also a happening college town, operating five universities including the University of California, Santa Barbara; Antioch University; and Brooks Institute of Photography. Families and students relax on Stearns Wharf, and thousands attend the annual French Festival and Summer Solstice Parade. One of the least visited of America's national parks is the Channel Islands, a nature preserve and isolated chain of islands in the Pacific. The Santa Ynez Mountains offer hikers and photographers miles of unspoiled terrain, vistas, and rushing waterfalls. Springtime brings spiky purple lupines, sticky monkey flower, and bright orange fields of the California poppy, the official California state flower.

Abandoned long ago, the Dining Cars Cafe sits stranded on an old road just off of U.S. Hwy. 101, north of Buellton. Opening as Mullen's Dining Cars in 1946, the cars went into service in 1911, running until WWII, when they were probably sold off for scrap.

Miss Teen California 2010, Dedria Brunet, posing next to a fine Auburn Boattail Speedster at National Car Collector Appreciation Day 2011.

The vegetable fields just outside Lompoc.

The Neptune Pool went through several incarnations starting in 1924. This final version is 104 feet long, 58 feet wide, between 3.5 feet and 10 feet deep, and holds 435,000 gallons of water. The Roman Pool is comprised of 1" square mosaic glass tiles called *smalti*. This pool was modeled after the Roman Baths of Caracalla (c. A.D. 211-17). Another source of inspiration was the Mausoleum of Galla Placidia, a fifth-century structure with marble walls, vaulted arches, and blue and gold smalti covering all surfaces. *Photo by Adriene Biondo.*

William Randolph Hearst inherited this 250,000-acre ranch just outside of San Luis Obispo from his wealthy parents in 1919. It started out as a place for camping, but Hearst wanted something a bit more comfortable, so he hired San Francisco architect Julia Morgan to "...build a little something." By 1947, the estate had 165 rooms and 127 acres of gardens, terraces, pools, and walkways. It was so lavish that it was a model for Orson Welles' classic film *Citizen Kane* dubbed "Xanadu." The Hearst Corporation donated "The Enchanted Hill" to the State of California in December 1959, when it became a State Historical Monument. *Photo by Adriene Biondo.*

A typical Parisian posing proudly in front of the Eiffel Tower, albeit Paris via
Santa Barbara...and the Eiffel Tower a scale model made of re-bar.

This Mission in Santa Barbara stands as a historic reminder of the Old Spanish
Missions of the past. In 1869, Father Junipero Serra built the first Mission in San
Diego. During the following years, many more missions were constructed between
San Diego and Sonoma, each only one day's journey from the next.

PREVIOUS PAGE
Apparently, Tahiti was a big part of the French Empire at one time. Here a lovely
Tahitian dancer reminds us just how much.

A milestone French invention was the guillotine, originally designed as a merciful way
of performing an execution. Here a tourist appears happy to test the sharpness of the
blade.

Another unique invention of the French is the Can-Can, demonstrated here by a group
of beautiful young ladies performing during the 2010 French Festival in Santa Barbara.

Now here's a town steeped in tradition and windmills. The City of Solvang (Danish for "sunny fields") offers a taste of Denmark all year 'round with more than one million visitors a year. Since the 2004 movie *Sideways*, filmed in nearby Santa Ynez Valley, we sure have seen a lot more wine shops crop up in town.

Sam Liberty was present during this 4th of July celebration when the Independence Day parade took over the town of Carpinteria. We think the entire town participated along with additional attractions borrowed from nearby Santa Barbara, not to mention the U.S. Navy. 2010 Rods n' Roses Parade, Carpinteria.

Proud U.S. Navy members joined the parade which went on for hours.

Fireworks on the 4th of July. *Photo by Adriene Biondo.*

From the comfort of Pismo Bowl in the heart of town, spectators can admire classic cars cruising the streets between knocking down bowling pins.

Even a kid with a swanky mohawk was on display.

At the Pismo Beach car show, hundreds of vintage cars promenaded down Main Street in front of *oohing* and *aaahing* onlookers.

Muscle cars, customs, classics, and rides of all types made it an enjoyable family day.

For the most dramatic effect, the Hot Air Balloon and Wine Festival in Santa Paula waited for sunset before prepping for lift-off.

Here, the balloons are inflated with hot gas via burners that sounded like jet engines. Interestingly enough, many of the baskets are made of wicker.

After dark, the balloons were lit in sync to music in a spectacular display that thrilled the crowd.

You can always find an automotive event going on in Southern California. A favorite is the Primer Nats at the Ventura County Fairgrounds, where classics, customs, hot rods, vintage trailers, and rockabilly bands all come together for a fun-filled weekend. 2010 Primer Nationals, Ventura.

Finalists in the hair design contest show off in true retro style.

Although the *official* fireworks show in the skies of Fillmore during the 4th of July was awesome; the show on the ground, was equally amazing in this small farming community. This town *loves* their pyrotechnics. Cars were dodging fireworks throughout the streets, we didn't just see a fireworks show, we had an unforgettable 4th of July *experience*.

A fixture at Ventura harbor, this custom-built Chinese junk can be chartered for parties and overnight stays.
Photo by Adriene Biondo.

An afternoon view of the busy Ventura harbor, where many sailors (and landlubbers) make their home.

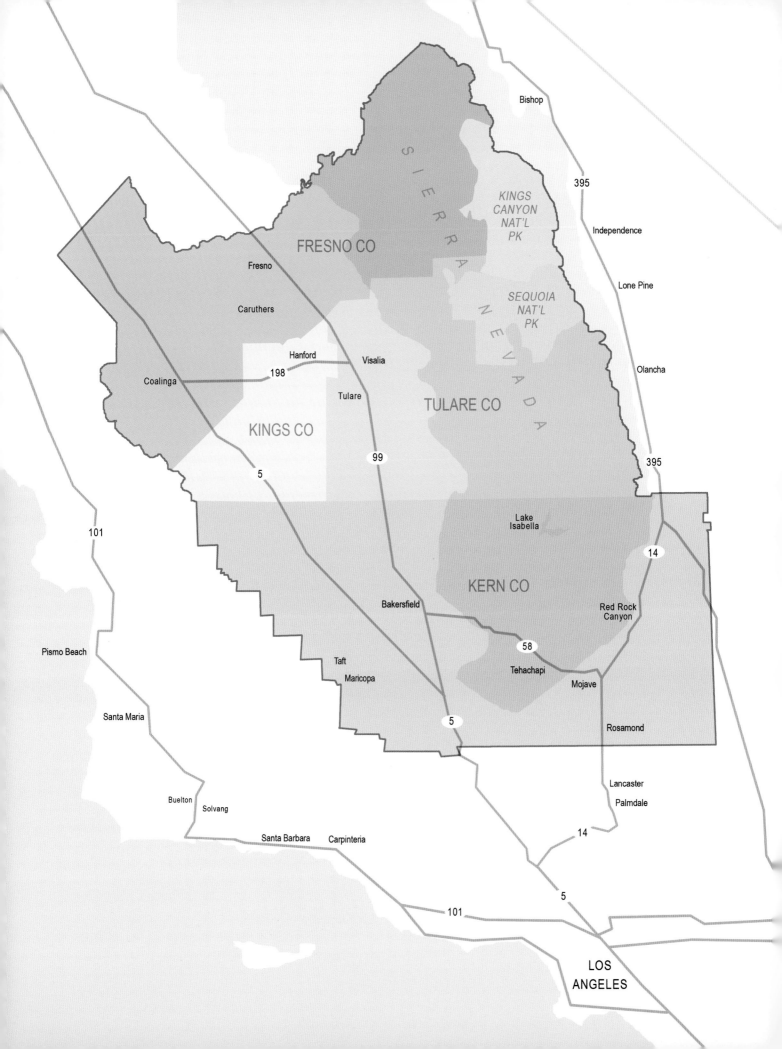

3 Central Valley & Western Sierra

In Sequoia National Park, near Lodgepole, this tree was deliberately left here just to remind visitors how large giant redwoods really are, so large you can actually drive through them! The *Sequoia gigantea* (big tree, or Sierra redwood) are amongst the largest and oldest living organisms in the world.

"I thought of the palmy islands of the Pacific, of the plains of Mexico, and of the Andes of Peru, but the attractions of California were yet stronger than all others, and I decided to stay another year or two."

–John Muir

"...go to the mountains and get the good tidings...and nature's peace will flow into you like sunshine into trees."

–John Muir

The Central Valley is roughly 450 miles long and 40-60 miles wide. This flat region that runs down the middle of the state is known as the Sacramento Valley to the north and the San Joaquin Valley to the south. Here, in the farmlands, fields, and roadside produce stands, one quarter of the food Americans eat is grown: grapes, citrus fruits, apricots, asparagus, tomatoes, almonds, and grains. Kings County is located in the south central San Joaquin Valley's rich agricultural area, along with the county seat, the historic town of Hanford. Almost directly in the center of the state is Fresno County, which is Spanish for "ash tree," and is also known as the "Raisin Capital of the World." South of Fresno is Tulare County with beautiful Sequoia National Park and the county seat of Visalia. Extending east beyond the southern slope of the Sierra Nevada is Kern County, California's top oil-producing county.

One of the primary sources of water for agriculture and the cities of California is from the melting snow of the Sierra Nevada mountain range directly east. Named by the Spanish in the seventeenth century, Sierra Nevada means "snowy ranges." This mountain range is similar in shape to the state and is approximately 400 miles in length with an average of 70 miles in width. Here you can find many peaks above 14,000 feet and some of the most magnificent scenery in the world. The crown jewels of the Sierra Nevada are Yosemite, Kings Canyon, and Sequoia National Park. Redwood trees are the official state tree and many in Sequoia are more than 2,000 years old. The redwood is also among the tallest, some growing to 370 feet tall. Their roots, however, grow very shallow, approximately 10 feet deep. That is why even on short hikes, you will come across many trees that have simply tipped over from being top heavy. The California Aqueduct in the Central Valley brings Sierra Nevada water to the farmlands of this region as well as Los Angeles, further south.

Most of the land in the Sierra Nevada range is owned by the U.S. government and protected from development. The three agencies that manage the recreation and development of this land are the National Park Service, under the Secretary of the Interior; the National Forest Service, under the Secretary of Agriculture; and the Bureau of Land Management (BLM). Early surveyor Clarence King wrote about his 1864 explorations with the California Geological Survey. John Muir preached the gospel of nature throughout the late 1800s and was principal in forming the Sierra Club, a group interested in exploring, enjoying, and preserving wild places, starting in California's Sierra Nevada.

CENTRAL VALLEY
& WESTERN SIERRA

Dramatic afternoon clouds over the agricultural fields in the sprawling San Joaquin Valley.

The historic Hanford Auditorium in the quaint all-American town of Hanford.

Mearle's Drive-In, built in 1940, became a rite of passage for teens growing up in
the farming town of Visalia, gateway to the Sequoia National Park. Mearle's narrowly
escaped the wrecking ball and has been resurrected as The Habit Grill.

Sometimes clues to the past for an urban archeologist
are in plain sight. Kern Drugs, Bakersfield.

Got shoe? We love this rare Programmatic building that is still operating as a shoe repair shop! No need for a GPS when you can see the giant shoe a full block away. Stop in and bring your tired, worn-out shoes—let's keep this place going!

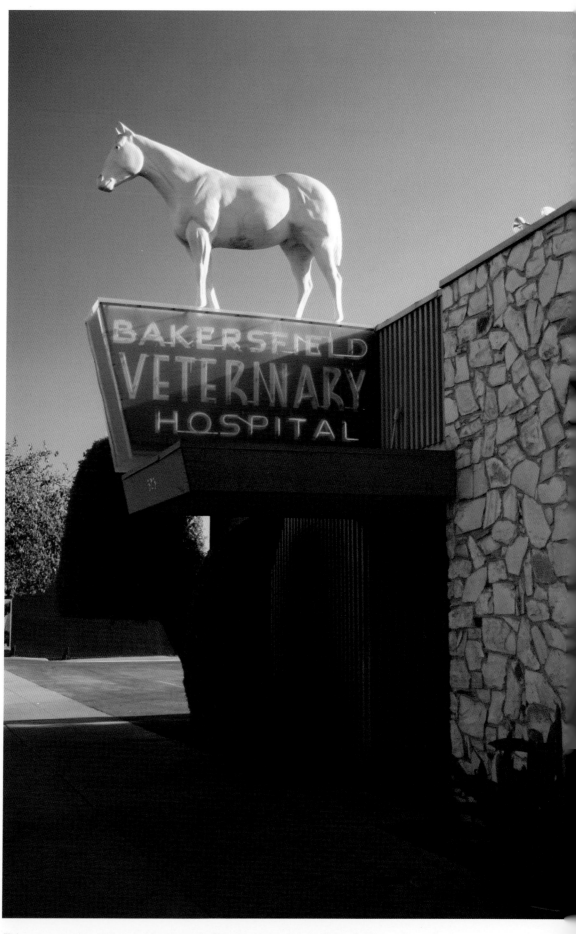

Things come and go. We took this photo of a fiberglass horse atop the Bakersfield Veterinary Hospital just weeks before it was taken down.

We spotted this giant red ant, looking very hungry, on a farm just outside of Tehachapi.

A rare World War II bomber gas station in the rural farming town of Caruthers.

Monument to the Oil Men, the early pioneers of Taft. According to local historian Pete Gianopulos, "...Taft resembled a mining town that never slept."

They've been called many things, from "mules" to "donkeys." Whatever you like to call these pumping units, they work 24/7, never sleep, eat, or complain.

The Oilworker, by sculptor Benjamin Victor, celebrates the 100-year anniversary of oil in the City of Taft in 2010. Even now, California is the third biggest producer of oil in the U.S., after Alaska and Texas.

A late 1950s bowling alley left over from the last mid-century's bowling boom. The atomic elements of this ultra-modern bowling alley are still very obvious. Since bowling is certainly not what it used to be, let's keep an eye on this place. Cedar Lanes, Bakersfield.

Downtown Fresno, a unique early urban shopping district designed by world renowned architect Victor Gruen and Associates in the early 1960s.

Old China Alley, Fresno. In 1874, 600 settlers, 200 of which were Chinese, moved to what has become Fresno.

Vintage neon, this La Fiesta sign is in one of the oldest sections of Fresno, near Chinatown.

Atlas sculpture, Bakersfield.

One of the native local residents of Sequoia National Park greeting tourists. His home of Sequoia and Kings Canyon covers an area roughly 66 by 36 miles or 865,257 acres. As lovable as they may appear, do not feed the animals. Keep them wild.

Hikers returning from a backpacking trip in Sequoia National Park, established in 1890 as the second National Park in the nation, after Yellowstone. Here, there are more than 800 miles of marked trails, more than 1,200 campsites and accommodations, thousands of species of plants, and hundreds of species of animals.

This vista of Farewell Canyon greets you along the trail just south of
Sawtooth Peak in the Mineral King region of Sequoia National Park.

OPPOSITE PAGE
In Sequoia National Park, giant sequoia trees can be found along with sugar pine,
white fir, and red fir (also extremely large). The most famous of these sequoia
trees is General Sherman, which stands at 275 feet with a base diameter of
more than 35 feet. Recognized as the largest tree in the world, it is estimated to
be between 2,300 and 2,700 years old. Visiting these massive living wonders of
nature will not disappoint.

The surreal landscape of Red Rock, north of the town Mojave, has stood in for alien landscapes in sci-fi and western movies alike.

Approaching storm in the farmlands of the San Joaquin Valley, just east of Taft.

4 Eastern Sierra & Central Desert

Heading east towards Mono Lake from Tioga Pass Road. The vistas from here are out of this world.

EASTERN SIERRA &
CENTRAL DESERT

"A strange thing happened to me today. I saw a big thundercloud move down over Half Dome, and it was so big and clear and brilliant that it made me see many things...For the first time *I know* what love is; what friends are; and what art should be."

–Ansel Adams in a letter to Cedric Wright, June 1937

Starting from the north, Mono County is among the highest, harshest, wildest, remotest, and most inhospitable places in North America, but it is also among the most beautiful and sublime. There are no major cities in this region but it is teeming with life—wildlife.

High on the White Mountain range, above 10,000 feet, you can find one of the oldest living organisms in the world. Some of the ancient bristlecone pines have been around for 4,600 years, with the oldest being Methuselah, reported to be 4,723 years old.

Mono Lake has a unique ecology unlike just about anything else on this planet. One of the most striking elements of this 700,000-year-old lake are the "tufa" towers which are easily found along the southern beaches. Over time, the calcium from underground springs combined with the carbonate in the water and formed limestone spires known as "tufa towers."

Bodie, a State Historical Park and museum, is known as "America's Best-Preserved Ghost Town." Protected mainly by its remote location, visiting this town is actually *better* than using a time machine because it is safer.

Along Interstate 395, just south of Lee Vining, you'll find Tioga Pass Road, which will bring you up to almost 10,000 feet and into the northeast entrance of Yosemite National Park. Here is mountain scenery that will touch your soul.

The next county south is Inyo County, an agricultural community during the late 1800s. Inyo County changed to recreation and tourism during the first quarter of the twentieth century. At this time, the City of Los Angeles bought most of the water rights in this region in order to build the 233-mile L.A. Aqueduct. Here, along the Sierra Nevada crest, many peaks stand over 14,000 feet, including Mount Whitney at 14,495 feet (the highest in the lower 48s). Less than 80 miles southeast is Death Valley, with Badwater, the lowest place in the U.S. at 282 feet *below* sea level.

Further south, San Bernardino County, at three million acres, is the largest county in the entire United States. Part of the famous Route 66 runs through this county. It is mainly known for its agriculture, universities, recreation, and unique desert environment. During World War II, the desert region east of Joshua Tree National Park was personally picked by General George Patton as the training ground for more than a million troops heading to North Africa. Now, there are still a number of military bases in China Lake, Mojave, Joshua Tree, and the Chocolate Mountains.

Remember Magic Rocks when you were growing up? Multiply that by a trillion. Some things are stranger than fiction. These tufa formations along Navy Beach at Mono Lake are both striking and surreal. If we hadn't seen these with our own eyes, we would have given Photoshop more credit than it deserves. These are real, go see them.

North Peak (12,242 ft.) from Secret Lake. The Twenty Lakes Basin along the Sierra Crest has been described as our local Shangri-La and is one of the best-kept secrets of the High Sierra, so don't tell anyone.

Ice cave found along the Twenty Lakes Basin trail. This region is incredibly accessible thanks to Tioga Pass Road, which brings travelers up to nearly 10,000 feet. Originally a private mining road, Steven Mathers, the first superintendent of the National Parks, bought it for $15,000 in 1915 with mostly his own money. He then donated it to the National Parks system so that everyone would be able to enjoy the High Sierra.

Mono Lake Tufa State Reserve. A crimson sky reflected off the serene waters of the lake. Sublime is not an inappropriate description of this special lake which has infinite moods depending on the climate and light. A photographer's heaven that we never get tired of visiting.

Canoers enjoying an early morning paddle just after sunrise on Mono Lake. Once underwater, these surrealistic spires were created by the calcium and carbonates in the highly salty water.

Bridgeport Inn, a local haunt, and we mean literally. There's a plaque telling the whole story and which rooms ghosts have been seen in. This town has another hotel which was once a bordello in Bodie that is also known for paranormal activity.

The stunning Mono County Courthouse at Bridgeport is still in use today. It is the second oldest continuously used County Courthouse in the State of California. The two-story Italianate style structure was built in 1880.

Thousand Island Lakes looking toward Mt. Ritter and Banner Peak, both under a rising cloud cover that had just dumped three inches of snow on us.

A hiker crossing Glen Pass (11,978 ft.), just south of Rae Lakes along the John Muir Trail.

Autumn color with aspen trees aglow off Rock Creek near Tom's Place.
Visitors can pick up a driving guide to the best areas to view fall color.

One of our favorite places on Earth, Woods Lodge at Lake George in Mammoth.

Minarets on the trail near Thousand Island Lakes.

Watching over Lake George in Mammoth is Crystal Crag, an impressive
peak reminiscent of the Matterhorn when viewed from this angle.

Like a sentinel greeting visitors, a giant rusting flywheel sits at the entrance of Bodie. A State Historic Park and National Park, Bodie is one of the largest unrestored ghost towns in the American West. During its most profitable mining era between 1877-1888, Bodie is said to have had 10,000 residents and yielded a phenomenal $35 million in gold and silver.

Stamped metal panels rusting in the harsh elements of Bodie.

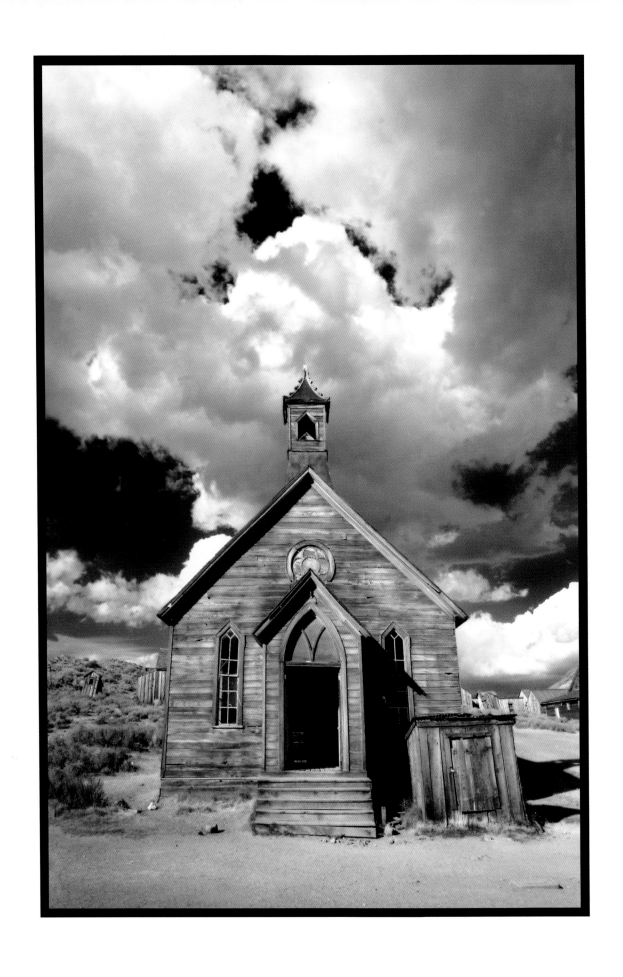

Apparently a church was much needed in Bodie...known as one of the most lawless Wild West towns, rife with gambling, prostitution, and stories of people gunned down in the middle of its streets.

An outhouse in Bodie, where things are preserved in "a state of arrested decay." Don't forget to bring your own toilet paper.

A mutation in nature: Siamese twins attached at the head. Display exhibited at the Laws Museum just north of Bishop.

Gateway Motel in the town of Lee Vining, gateway to Yosemite via Tioga Pass to the west, Mono Lake to the east, and Bodie and Bridgeport to the north.

Sand dunes at Stovepipe, Death Valley, a location
used in many movies including Erich Von Stroheim's
silent classic, *Greed* (1925).

Sage Motel in Needles, on the border of California and Arizona. On this day it was 120 degrees, not all that unusual for this area. We didn't notice an AAA rating.

A local checking his mail at the post office in Pioneertown, five miles north of Yucca Valley. The name "Pioneertown" was inspired by famed cowboy star Roy Rogers and his Sons of the Pioneers, a bunch of singing cowboys, in the 1940s.

An abandoned garage on Route 66 in Ludlow; a sad reminder of an era gone by.

What is the attraction to these transitory, obsolete, desolate structures? Interior of the garage at Ludlow.

Roy's Motel out in the Mojave Desert on Route 66 in Amboy. This section of Route 66 is pretty much abandoned due to the bypass by Interstate 40. The town of Amboy is now owned by Roy Okura of Juan Pollo restaurants who purchased the entire town after a failed auction on eBay.

Welcome Space Brothers and Sisters! This circa 1950s rotunda was built by George Van Tassel, former aerospace engineer and test pilot who was employed by Lockheed Aircraft and Howard Hughes. The story behind this extraterrestrial connection is a classic example of why some wryly refer to California as "the land of fruits and nuts."

After moving to Twentynine Palms in 1947, Van Tassel is said to have become enlightened, and in 1953 was reportedly visited by *Solganda*, a space alien who appeared at the foot of his bed, to indoctrinate him to the technology and plans to slow aging and recharge our body's cells by building this parabolic dome known as "The Integratron." Today, visitors can learn all about George and luxuriate in a sound bath. Landers, just north of Yucca Valley.

Most people know about the Los Angeles Aqueduct that brings water from the Eastern Sierra's Owens Valley to L.A. because of the various legal battles (and the movie *Chinatown*), but there is another aqueduct that many are unaware of, even native-born Angelenos. The Colorado River Aqueduct was the project of the Metropolitan Water District of Southern California between 1933-1941 that delivers clean drinking water to Southern California cities from the Colorado River. Starting at Lake Havasu and ending in Los Angeles, this aqueduct stretches 242 miles across the Mojave Desert via a series of pumping plants, tunnels, canals, siphons, transmission lines, dams, and reservoirs. In 1955, it was designated one of the Seven Modern Civil Engineering Wonders in the U.S.

Inside the Metropolitan Water District intake pumping plant at Lake Havasu. As the first step in filtering silt, Parker Dam raised the water level from 72 feet to 450 feet, creating a reservoir called Lake Havasu, also in use today as a recreation center.

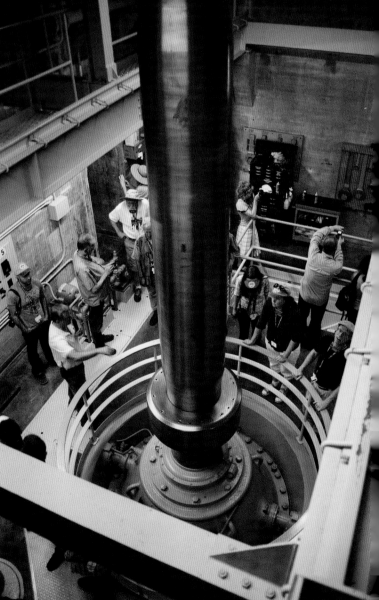

MOJAVE DESERT

Twentynine
Palms

LOS
ANGELES

Riverside   Cabazon   JOSHUA TREE NT'L PK

215   Palm   10   Desert
Springs   Coachella   Center

Fullerton
Anaheim
Orange
ORANGE
CO   Perris   Hemet   Idyllwild   SAN
JACINTO
MOUNTAIN   RIVERSIDE CO   10   Blythe

Newport Beach   5

Temecula   Salton Sea   Niland

IMPERIAL CO

Oceanside   15   Escondido   Anza
Borrego
Desert
State
Park   SAN DIEGO
CO   Brawley

5   8
SAN
DIEGO   Calexico   8

5 Southern Coast & Southern Desert

Surfer at the Oceanside Pier, Oceanside.

"The formula for a happy marriage? It's the same as the one for living in California: When you find a fault, don't dwell on it."

–Jay Trachman

Everybody knows that Orange County is Disneyland country. But it doesn't end there. Sand. Surfing. Skateboarding. Angel Stadium. Medieval Times. Knotts Berry Farm. The Balboa Island Ferry. And then there's Laguna...for more than seventy years, the arts colony of Laguna Beach has presented its Festival of Arts and Pageant of the Masters, a proud tradition of the City of Laguna Beach. One of the nicest walking towns is San Juan Capistrano, with OC's only mission, historic adobes, gardens, galleries, and souvenir shops.

Whenever you think of Riverside County, you think of the romantic Mission Inn. Built over a thirty-year period in a variety of architectural styles, this magnificent resort hotel features castle towers, gargoyles, catacombs, a rotunda, a Medieval style clock, a pedestrian skyway, and much more. Two of the finest transportation museums are also in the area, the Orange Empire Railway Museum in Perris, and the March Field Air Museum at March Air Force Base (open to the public). And last but certainly not least is…Palm Springs, Southern California's most luxurious destination and desert resort. Here you can bask in the Southern California sun and dream of Frank Sinatra and Ava Gardner strolling through town back in the Golden Age of Hollywood.

San Diego County is known for having the best climate in the world. From amusement parks like Lego Land to the world-famous Sea World and the San Diego Zoo to museums like the Old Globe Theatre at Balboa Park, San Diego has more than just a great climate. Take a trolley over to Horton Plaza, then head over to the historic Gaslamp Quarter for dinner and entertainment. In Old Town San Diego, you'll have a chance to re-live San Diego circa 1820-1870, tour a blacksmith's shop, and see San Diego's first newspaper office. You won't want to miss the haunted Whaley House or see the Victorian homes at Heritage Park Victorian Village.

Imperial County borders Mexico and Arizona and is primarily a dry desert irrigated by the Colorado River. Take a drive to the enigmatic Salton Sea and learn all about its history at the newly restored Salton Sea History Museum and Visitor's Center. Continue on for an unusual and uplifting pilgrimage to Salvation Mountain. Photographers will also enjoy visiting picturesque Anza-Borrego Desert State Park and the Algodones Dunes, the largest area of sand dunes in California.

SOUTHERN COAST & SOUTHERN DESERT

Sleeping Beauty Castle, beloved symbol of Disneyland, opened July 17, 1955. The castle was designed by Disney Imagineer Herb Ryman and inspired by the Neuschwanstein Castle in Germany. Here she is restored and resplendent in a new coat of finery celebrating Disneyland's 50th anniversary.

Disneyland's "It's a Small World" ride in Fantasyland was designed by Mary Blair. It originally made its debut at the 1964 New York World's Fair. It is one of five attractions that was moved to Disneyland after the World's Fair closed in 1966.

A stunning mid-century modern tract home in one of the famed Eichler tracts in Orange County.

This crew of the U.S.S. *Enterprise* from the TV series *Star Trek* never ages...but they do melt. Movieland Wax Museum, Buena Park. Photo taken just before the Wax Museum was decommissioned and auctioned off. Though this one has closed, the Hollywood Wax Museum is still going strong. *Photo by Adriene Biondo.*

Wax clan of the TV show *The Beverly Hillbillies*. The good fortune of Jed Clampett and his family has finally run out as they are evicted from their Beverly Hills mansion in Buena Park. *Photo by Adriene Biondo.*

Crystal Cathedral, with more than 10,000 windows of tempered silver glass, is a tour de force combining the architectural genius of Philip Johnson and John Burgee. Reverend Robert H. Schuller started his church in 1955 in a Garden Grove parking lot, preaching to folks in their cars, drive-in style without any walls or ceiling. Through the years it has grown into a mega church until 2011, when the church filed for bankruptcy.

View of the Coachella Valley with the Morongo Casino at center. Image taken while driving down San Jacinto Mountain from Idyllwild.

A scene out of *1001 Arabian Nights* and home of Queen Scheherazade and Her Court. In 2010—its 65th year—the Riverside County Fair and National Date Festival set a record-breaking attendance record, drawing more than 300,000 visitors.

The magnificent Mission Inn has hosted presidents, royalty, and celebrities over its lifetime. Christopher Columbus Miller began with a modest 12-room adobe, then his son Frank Miller continued construction, hiring a number of architects who transformed the Inn over the next 66 years. Its eclectic design is picturesque and romantic, combining Moorish and Spanish styles. Fascinating history, and a must-see if ever you're ever near Riverside!

The 6-story Rotunda of the Mission Inn, Riverside, often listed as the most beautiful and interesting thing to see in Riverside County. And who are we to disagree?

Family sneaking a peek at the new dinosaur display at Cabazon, now owned by an Intelligent Design Group. The original Cabazon dinosaurs were designed by Claude Bell, of Knotts Berry Farm fame.

This giant VW spider lurks at the front entry of Hole in the Wall Welding in Indio. Luckily it moves very slowly so you'll have time to get away.

March Air Field Aviation Museum in Perris displays a fine collection of aircraft. Aside from this giant World War II-era KC-97L Stratofreighter, there are modern jets such as the SR-71 Blackbird.

P-40 Warhawk, a classic World War II fighting machine, at the entrance of the March Air Field, Perris.

1
An old school barber in the border town of Blythe.
He collects old postcards of Blythe. Ironically, in
order to get what he wants, he has to look on eBay.

2
We ran across a troupe of Civil War reenactors in
the town of Banning.

3
Agriculture has been a vital California industry for
more than a century. Thanks to irrigation, even parts
of the barren Mojave Desert have been converted
to productive farmlands, like this one west of Blythe.

4
An Elvis impersonator performing at the Perris Train
Festival, Perris.

3

Algodones Dunes in the Imperial Valley was used by George Lucas as a desert planet landscape in the movie *Return of the Jedi*.

Mile-high Palomar Observatory. At 5,500 feet and 45 miles from San Diego, the observatory has ideal conditions for observing the nighttime sky, away from city lights.

The 200-inch reflector telescope was constructed at Cal-Tech and installed in the Observatory in 1947.

The newly restored Visitor's Center at Salton Sea was originally the Salton Sea North Shore Beach and Yacht Club, designed by renowned Palm Springs architect Albert Frey in 1960.

For eons, the Salton Sea was nothing more than a sandy depression and part of prehistoric Lake Cahuilla. In 1905, the desert sink was filled due to an accidental overflow of the Colorado River. Two years later, the 45 mile long by an average of 12 mile wide body of water became known as the Salton Sea. During the 1950s and 60s, Salton Sea briefly became a thriving resort for Southern California vacation-goers.

A typical home in Palm Springs, a magnificent mid-century modern mecca of Southern California.

Former Coachella Valley Savings and Loan Association (1960), E. Stewart Williams architect, one of Palm Springs most enduring commercial landmarks.

Shields Date Farm opened back in 1924, becoming a charming rest stop and time capsule experience for the weary roadside traveler who desperately needs a refreshing Date Shake.

You can still see Mr. Shields' film, *Romance & Sex Life of the Date*, documenting how date palms are grown and harvested at Shields Date Farm. This controversial presentation has not changed since the 1950s and you still have to walk through the date shop in order to get a seat in the Romance Theater.

View of the giant sculptural relief "map" constructed by Metropolitan Water engineers in order to sell the idea of transporting water from the Colorado River to Los Angeles and adjacent counties. The survey team worked six years to determine the best route for this aqueduct. According to The Big Map brochure, the map "weighs close to five tons and is designed to come apart like a giant zigsaw puzzle." George Patton Museum, near Desert Center.

A World War II-era tank at the George Patton Memorial Museum. This was the desert area that Patton picked to train more than a million soldiers before they were shipped to North Africa during World War II.

Founded in 1775, Mission San Juan Capistrano was the 7th mission established by Father Junipero Serra. In 1812, the church was destroyed by an earthquake, sending its 120-foot tower smashing down upon the congregation and killing 43 Native Americans.

Flowering lilies in the pond at San Juan Capistrano. Capistrano is famous for the ritual of the swallows who faithfully return in tremendous numbers year after year on March 19th. They make their home here in summertime, departing October 23rd.

1

3

4

2

5

6

A surfer studying the waves on the beach of Oceanside.

Capri VILLA CAPRI MOTEL ENTRANCE

The Berkeley (1898), once a steam ferryboat, now the Maritime Museum of San Diego, and the U.S.S. *Dolphin* (1968), the deepest diving submarine in the world. San Diego Harbor.

The perfectly preserved Villa Capri Motel, across from the Hotel Del.

The elite seaside Hotel Del Coronado, designed by Stanford White in 1880; one of the most popular destinations in San Diego, or anywhere.

This gorgeous hotel was prominently showcased in the comedy classic *Some Like It Hot* (1959) with Marilyn Monroe, Tony Curtis, and Jack Lemmon, and in the 1980 film, *The Stuntman*.

Built for the 1915-16 and 1935-36 Pan Pacific International Exposition, Balboa Park now functions as the main Cultural and Recreational center for San Diego.

This 1,400-acre park includes gardens, museums, a band shell, a zoo, and much much more. Many of the buildings in this park were designed in the Spanish Renaissance style.

Star of India, the world's oldest active sailing ship, was built of iron in the Isle of Man in 1863. Now a permanent attraction at San Diego Harbor.

Bibliography

Books

Banham, Reyner. *Los Angeles The Architecture of Four Ecologies*. (New York: Penguin Books, 1971).

Davis, Erik and Michael Rauner. *The Visionary State, A Journey Through California's Spiritual Landscape*. (San Francisco: Chronicle Books, 2006).

Editors of California Department of Parks & Recreation. *The Visitor's Guide to California State Parks*. (Sacramento: Sequoia Communications, 1990).

Editors of Sunset Books and Sunset Magazine. *Beautiful California*. (Menlo Park: Lane Magazine & Book Company, 1963).

Editors of Sunset Books and Sunset Magazine. *Los Angeles Portrait of an Extraordinary City*. (Menlo Park: Lane Magazine & Book Company, 1973).

Gebhard, David and Robert Winter. *Los Angeles, An Architectural Guide*. (Salt Lake City: Gibbs-Smith Publisher, 1994).

Irwin, Sue, *California's Eastern Sierra A Visitor's Guide*. (Los Olivos: Cachuma Press, Inc., 1991).

Kaplan, Sam Hall. *L.A. Lost & Found*. (New York: Crown Publishers, Inc., 1987).

Koenig, Gloria, *Iconic LA, Stories of LA's Most Memorable Buildings*. (Glendale: Balcony Press, 2000).

Neuenburg, Evelyn. *California Lure The Golden State In Pictures*. (Pasadena: California Lure Publishers, 1946).

Phoenix, Charles. *Southern California in the '50s*. (Santa Monica: Angel City Press, 2001).

Shippey, Lee and Max Yavno. *The Los Angeles Book*. (Cambridge: Houghton Mifflin Company Boston, The Riverside Press, 1950).

Tom Harrison Maps. (San Rafael: tomharrisonmaps.com).

Welles, Annette. *The Los Angeles Guide Book*. (Los Angeles: Sherbourne Press, 1972).

Websites

astroluxe.org
California Travel and Tourism Commission
charlesphoenix.com
collectornetwork.net
hearstcastle.org
imdb.com
laconservancy.org
monolake.org
mwdh2o.com
parks.ca.gov
preservationnation.org
psmodcom.org
roadsidepeek.com
sierraclub.org
wikipedia.org

Late afternoon thunder storm over the San Joaquin Valley.

Acknowledgments

To everyone who inspired us along the way with their encouragement, advice and stories...from friends and family who sat in on slide shows of our adventures, to forest service rangers who helped direct us to incredible vistas in the High Sierras: John Biondo, Sr., John Biondo, Jr., Curt Cragg, Frank Donadee, Albert and Chui Yim Eng, Laura Friedman, Jeffrey Head, Hillary Hunter, Joe Langman, Jack and Jan Laxer, Guillaume Lemoine, Chris Nichols, Charles Phoenix, William "Skeeter" Rader, Stan Schotz, Dick Shelley, Drew Smith and Laura Massino-Smith, Gregg Townsend, Jim and Lori Tucci, Leon and Ann Tucci, Arlene Vidor, Gene Ward, Justeen Ward, Marty Ward, Kurt Zendler, and the person who returned our camera at the Long Beach Flea Market! And how could we go on any of these road trips without the help of Dan and Ann Ziliak, who always take good care of Poky, Cody, and Betty for us.

Sunset at Malibu.

Photo by Tom Eng.

Photo by John Eng.

About the Authors

John Eng is a writer, director, designer, and photographer living in Los Angeles. He grew up in Queens, New York, and attended The Brooklyn Museum Art School, Parsons School of Design, and The School of Visual Arts. After relocating to Los Angeles in 1981, he produced and shot live-action, independent feature films in addition to animation work in promos and television commercials. During the 1990s, John directed numerous animated television shows including *Duckman* and *Jonny Quest*. After 2000, John worked in both feature and TV animation. Projects include *Rugrats Go Wild, Jimmy Neutron, The Barnyard, Hoodwinked 2, Alpha and Omega, Curious George 2,* and *Lionelville*. His photography has appeared in *LA Magazine, Dwell, CA Modern* magazine, *Stern Magazine*, and his own website: astroluxe.org. John is currently shooting a documentary celebrating the 100th anniversary of the Sierra Club's Angeles Chapter.

A preservationist and photographer, Adriene is on the Board of Trustees of the Museum of Neon Art and is Chair Emeritus of the Los Angeles Conservancy's Modern Committee. She has worked with The Getty Conservation Institute, contributed to the Emmy-award winning video *SurveyLA* and written *Los Angeles: City of Tomorrow*, a publication for the National Trust. Adriene's work in the field of historic preservation combines her passions, from documenting the urban landscape to photography. Adriene has also co-authored three books with John Eng: *Southern California Eats 1 & 2* , and *Modern Tract Homes of Los Angeles*. Adriene and John live with their doggies Poky and Cody, and Betty the Turtle.

Superman chatting with a Hollywood local just outside Mann's (originally Grauman's) Chinese Theater.